THE SECRET TO A GREAT MUSIC MINISTRY

BibleLeague
CHICAGO, ILLINOIS

Other books in this series

The Secret to a
Great Preaching Ministry

The Secret to a
Great Discipleship Ministry

The Secret to a
Great Evangelism Ministry

The Secret to a
Great Leadership Ministry

The Secret to a Great Music Ministry

STEVEN ELZINGA

The Secret to a Great Music Ministry
By Steven Elzinga
Illustrations by Kirstin Vander Giessen-Reitsma

ISBN 1-882536-50-9

Printed in the United States of America, 2002

ACKNOWLEDGEMENTS

First of all I want to thank Mr. Lansingh. (That is what I call him, since he and I share the same first name.) You should thank him, too. He is responsible for keeping the book shorter than it might have been. He is responsible for making some sense out of passages that made sense to me but probably not to anyone else. Foremost, he is responsible for contributing a storyline to my thoughts, making the book a more lively read. Thanks, Steve.

Second, I would like to thank my wife. She sacrificed a two-day retreat because I was consumed with this burning question: What is music? She indulged my obsession. Thanks, Marie.

Third, I would like to thank my dad. A few years back he asked me to make tapes of his favorite hymns with the bass part on one track and the melody on the other. He then, on his own, learned the bass — proving that anyone can learn. (No offense, Dad.)

Last, I would like to thank God for giving us such a powerful, mysterious language of the heart that can bring us closer to Him and to each other.

CONTENTS

"You will sing psalms and hymns and spiritual songs among yourselves, making music to the Lord in your hearts."

— Ephesians 5:19, NLT

PREFACE

EVERY SUNDAY MORNING, MILLIONS OF BELIEVERS gather and sing. The music unites us, lifts us, and delivers our hearts to God. We leave behind our ordinary speech and embrace a unique language of worship.

Or, at least, that's how it should be. More and more, the modern church is finding its pews filled with those who are just watching, or only mouthing along. Those who have not been raised to sing are left out as mere spectators rather than participants.

The secret to a great music ministry lies in reaching these spectators. Success must be judged not by the quality of the musicians or the size of the crowd they draw, but by how many attenders are making music part of their daily life with God. The key is to get your on-stage music into homes.

This is a practical book filled with step-by-step ideas that you can implement — whether you are a pastor, a worship leader, part of the worship team, or a lay member of your church. With an audience of such varied musical knowledge, this book begins at square one with the question: Why is music important?

1

WHY IS MUSIC IMPORTANT?

ADELE WOKE, AS SHE DID EVERY MORNING, TO THE peals of bells coming from the city's cathedral. For all 12 years of her young life, her days had begun with the deep, resonating gongs luring her from her dreams. This morning she smiled at the sound and took notice. Adele walked to her window and watched the Notre Dame belltower as it played out its morning reveille against the backdrop of dawn.

She heard her parents stirring downstairs. Papa was starting the fires for his ovens, getting them ready to bake breads for the citizens of medieval Paris. Mama was beating out the floormats in the shop. She could almost hear them humming along to the tune of the bells, although she might have been imagining it.

When the last echo of the morning's song disappeared from Adele's ears, she got dressed and walked downstairs. The smells of yeast and butter already filled the rooms, as Papa had begun his baguettes and pastries. "So there you are," Mama said. "We're nearly out of Brie

and Camembert. After breakfast could you pick some up from the market?"

"Sure," Adele said absentmindedly. She picked up a cluster of grapes her mother had set on the table and began picking at it. "Mama, why do they play the bells at the church?"

"To tell us what time it is," she answered.

"But then why make it so beautiful?"

"Well," her mother said, pausing from scrubbing a large mixing bowl. "I suppose they want us to feel uplifted."

"What does 'uplift' mean?"

"Like — it raises our spirits, I guess."

Adele chewed on a grape and thought. "How does it do that?"

"I don't know, Adele. It just does," her mother said, then shouted into the next room. "Maurice! The baguettes — hurry up!"

Her father appeared at the door with an armful of day-old loaves and smiled at Adele. "Looks like you'll have the biggest breakfast in the world today!" She giggled.

"Papa, you tell me. Why do they play those songs every morning at the church?"

He sat down next to her at the table. "Ah, the bells. You know, some say the soul of the city is the toll of those bells." He paused to pluck a grape off her bunch. "We mark our lives by those songs, listening to them year after year. They tell us when to mourn a death, or when to celebrate a wedding. They surround us with beauty; they make us aware that God is always nearby. Without the bells I supposed we'd be lost."

"Oh," she smiled. That made a lot of sense ... but there was something she didn't quite get. "How can music do all that?"

"Well, you might try asking the bellringer himself," her father whispered conspiratorially. Adele caught the reprimanding glare directed at him from her mother.

"You should get to the market, Adele," she interrupted. "You can finish breakfast when you get back."

"All right, Mama," she sighed. Adele held on to her grapes and scooped up the money on the counter with her free hand. Within moments, her questions were forgotten as she headed out the door and shouted goodbye.

On Sunday morning, Adele sat with her parents inside Notre Dame and listened as the pipe organ's dense chords filled the cavernous cathedral with velvety waves of song. She was reminded all at once of her questions, not to mention the mysterious bellringer who was so cautiously mentioned. She thought of him high in the belfry, the unseen heart of the city, listening for once to another's hymn. Maybe he would know how music works, how a sequence of notes could have such meaning.

Adele made up her mind that she was going to find this bellringer and ask. She told her parents she wanted to sit in the back this morning. When they finally relented, she started toward the rear but then cut over to the left of the building. Her heart pounded as she imagined a thousand eyes bearing down on her, wondering where she was headed. She tried to look purposeful as she made her way to the stairway, as if 12-year-olds always ventured up to the dangerous walkways high above the city.

The climb up the stairs seemed to take eons as Adele worried about the echo of her footfalls. Hundreds of stairs she climbed, until at last the bright light of morning greeted her. It was soon joined by a host of gargoyles grimacing menacingly from their stone perches. Adele began to reconsider her impulsiveness as she struggled to tear her gaze from their horrid faces. But she had come this far. She edged along the narrow aisle with her eyes fixed upward on the belltowers, which soared into the vast vaults of the sky.

Adele noticed a quick movement in her peripheral vision. It seemed to have been near the south tower. When she lowered her eyes, she saw a door with a set of wooden stairs where the movement had been. Was this the bellringer she'd seen, or perhaps a refugee claiming sanctuary in the church? She rushed to the door, ignoring danger, and scampered up the stairs. She saw nothing but the gigantic bells — until her eyes adjusted to the darkened room and she could make out a shadowy figure behind a beam of wood.

"Are you the bellringer?"

The man made no movement, so she ventured, "Are you the one who wakes me every morning with those beautiful sounds?"

He turned toward Adele and stared intently at her. She could not tell if he looked with interest, skepticism, or anger, for his brow was so knotted with scars that they betrayed no emotion.

"I am."

"I love your bells," she quietly confessed. "I love how you play them."

Again, the man did not answer right away. He let the sound of Adele's voice echo in the small room. "Thank you," he answered.

Adele took this as an invitation to move closer to the bellringer. She could see worlds of pain and worlds of wisdom woven into his knotted skin, and her revulsion disappeared beneath awe.

"You know why music works, don't you?"

"Yes. I do."

"Will you tell me?"

The man closed his eyes. Adele wondered if that itself was an answer, but then he spoke. His words came out slowly, as if he considered each one carefully. "In order to understand how music affects people, you must first understand music." He said the word "music" as if it were life itself.

Adele nodded.

"Amazing grace!" the man shouted. Then, he breathed in a whisper, "how sweet the sound that saved a wretch like me." Silence filled the room. "Was that music?"

"No," Adele answered. Something about his choice of words seemed wrong to her. It nagged at the back of her mind, but she couldn't put her finger on it. "That was just talking."

"Correct. What would you need to make it into

music?"

"You need to say them with the right spacing in between."

"Ah. A beat. I have to pronounce each syllable on a certain beat. *Da-Dum. Da-Dum. How-Sweet. The-Sound.* But then, adding a beat to words does not make the words spring into music. In fact, if you simply say words to a particular rhythm, what you end up with is poetry. So what else do you need?"

"Your voice has to go up and down."

"Changing pitch, yes. Of course, our voices always go up and down when we talk. In order for our pitch to become music, it has to follow some recognizable form — some relative distance between pitches."

"Like notes?"

"Exactly. Will just any notes do?" The bellringer screeched: "A-MAAAAA-ZING GRAAACE!"

"No, no," Adele laughed. "The right notes!"

"Ah, but how do you know what the right notes are?"

She hesitated. "You just do."

The man smiled. "It's a bit more complicated than that, but yes, you know the right notes because you and everyone around you *recognize* them as being right. Every time you hear 'Amazing Grace', it is the same words in the same order, said to the same beat, and always with the same relative pitches. This three-fold pattern becomes recognizable. And that's music in its most basic form: a recognizable pattern."

"All right," Adele murmured, absorbing his words. "But how does that make music so important to everyone in the city?"

"Indeed. If music is just a recognizable pattern, how can it lift your spirits? How can it sometimes bring you to tears? How can it bring back memories and feelings of long ago?" The bellringer motioned to a stack of wooden crates in the corner. "Perhaps we should sit down."

"Thank you," said Adele, as he set down crates for them.

"Let's try a little game. Do you remember what the priest talked about last Sunday?"

"I think so."

"And can you quote for me any of what he said?"

"Of course not!"

"That's because he said those words to you only once, and in no special order. A song, on the other hand, has a pattern. You hear it over and over. It has words that rhyme, and a certain number of syllables in each line. And so you can remember it."

"That seems obvious."

"But what isn't so obvious is that you remember more than just the notes and the words. You remember the places you learned them. You remember the people you sang them with. And because the pattern of music means that you will repeat it many times throughout your life, over time a song will gather many layers of meaning."

Adele's forehead wrinkled. "I'm not sure I understand."

"Let's make it personal, then. Did your mother ever sing you a lullaby?"

"Yes, there were many."

"Think of one. Try to remember the words."

It had been a long time since Adele thought of those songs. She struggled to latch onto the words. *Hush.* She tried to imagine herself in Mama's arms. *Hush now.* She could feel her face against her mother's shirt. She could smell the clean fabric. *Hush now, little one.* She could remember the feeling of being safe, of being warm, of being content.

"Do you remember?" the bellringer asked.

"Only a phrase so far. And a bit of the tune."

"And do you remember the feelings of having it sung to you?"

"Yes." Adele's eyes opened. "Oh, I see!"

"The easiest way to say it is that music is sticky. It catches memories. You hear someone sing a familiar song, and suddenly you smell smells, you feel feelings, you relive a whole era of your life — not just a memory of some past event, but the event itself.

"And not just the event. It can become more powerful than the actual first experience. The years will add layer upon layer of memories and feelings, good times and bad times, emotion upon emotion. When you are old and your mother has died, that lullaby is going to make you remember her, and so it will be both very sad and very sweet."

"All that from just a song?" Adele said.

"Yes," the bellringer answered, and looked away from Adele. She wondered what memories were racing through his mind. "Think of how people say 'that's music to my ears' — what they mean is, it's recreating these

pleasant, joyous feelings inside them. Because that's what music does."

He turned back to face her. "But we have only looked at half of the equation," he said. "Remember that the other component of music is being recognizable. Tell me, have you ever heard music from India?"

"I think so. In the marketplace. But it's not really that good."

"It doesn't sound right *to you*. But do you think it sounds good to them?"

"Probably."

"Why is that?"

"Because ... ," Adele said, "it's familiar to them."

"Exactly. And it's not familiar to you. You don't know the language; you don't understand the beat. And their pitches use a different musical scale than the one you are accustomed to. You don't recognize it. Whereas you and everyone around you recognize the notes of 'Amazing Grace.' Your particular style of music puts you into a certain group of people. So when I say that music requires recognizability, it really means that it connects you to other people."

"So ... the bells help unite the city because it's 'our' music?"

"Yes — you catch on quickly. Individual songs will be meaningful to individual people, but the genre of songs we surround ourselves with will define us as a group. It gives us identity and community. When I say that music is sticky, that's also because it binds us together."

"Sticky." Adele grinned.

"Certainly. Let's say you grow up and then move away to the countryside. You could live there 30 years and still, you would prefer to hear these old bells more than any other music. That's because it surrounded you during the most emotional time of your life — the time of life you were trying to figure out who you were, what you were going to do, and with whom you were going to do it. And you are stuck together with everyone else who loves the bells. In fact, I'd guess you'll never move out to the country at all, because your love for the bells has already made you a Parisian for life."

"Yes. Yes, I suppose it has." Adele stood up from her crate. "Thank you, sir," she said, extending her hand. "I think I understand now."

"Isn't there another question you want to ask?" the bellringer said, remaining seated.

Adele thought hard. "I don't know."

"I have explained what music is. I have told you how it moves us. I have yet to explain why music is so powerful."

Adele sat down again. "There's a why?"

"Of course. Who do you think created music?"

"God?"

"Yes. Music is like a special language that God created for us to speak to Him. I ring these bells every day because they resonate His glory more eloquently than I ever could with this tongue. And I think it can work the other way around, too. Sometimes when words and thoughts cannot console us, music can lift our hearts. It gives us that taste of the divine."

"Really?"

"Sure. Everything I've told you about music is part of God's plan for us as His people. When I said that music binds us together, it works with the church, too. The music that we make part of our life gives us identity; it makes us into a community as we learn to make music together. When I said that music catches memories, I think that's something God uses to remind us of all the times He's been with us through the years. Just as your lullaby can make you feel your mother's presence, so also a special song can make you feel wrapped up in God's arms."

Adele smiled. "I never thought of that."

"Songs are also a way for us to have God nearby us at all times. The Bible tells us to hide His words in our hearts, and song is a perfect way to do that because of its recognizable pattern. Some of my favorite songs are just passages from Scripture, and of course the book of Psalms is filled with nothing but songs to God. When you memorize these songs or passages, God can speak to you clearly by just bringing them to mind."

"I see — because the songs are sticky."

"Most people get upset when they get a song stuck in their head," the bellringer said, "but it can be quite useful!"

They both laughed.

"So how come more people don't talk to God and listen to God using music?" Adele asked.

"Let me ask: Do you know how to play an instrument?"

"No. Well, not very well."

The man nodded. "Most people are like you. Music is part of your life, but you don't know as much about it as you could. Remember how I said music is a language, of sorts, that God and people use to communicate? What would happen if you heard a language being spoken around you all the time, but you never tried to learn it?"

"I don't know. I suppose I'd pick up enough phrases to get by, but ... oh, I get it! I couldn't have a very good conversation with someone!"

"Indeed. The key to tapping into the spiritual power of music is in playing it, not just in listening. Like any language, it must be learned. The more you know, the more it does to you and for you. Suddenly, you are no longer a wallflower struggling to catch a phrase here and there, but a full participant, who can initiate conversation and listen attentively."

"So how can I learn music?"

"Well, most people learn by being born in a musical family, or by taking private lessons, or maybe from a friend who knows. But I don't believe that this gets the job done very effectively. Maybe there's a better way. What if the church, which spends half its service on music as it is, tried to teach you? What if there was a church out there interested in seeing you make music part of your life with God? What if it used its talented people and its music resources to help you?"

"Is there such a place?"

"To tell you the truth, I don't know. I haven't been outside this building much since I was a boy. But I have to imagine that somewhere out there, there's a church that has dared to try it."

"I sure hope so. I'd love to learn to make music myself."

The bellringer grinned. "Well, in the meantime, I suppose you've become enough of a friend that I can teach you a lesson or two." He got up from his crate and lumbered over to his giant metal instruments. "Come over to the bells and I'll teach you how to play 'Amazing Grace.'"

"In the middle of the service?" Adele gasped. "But they'll —"

Suddenly, what had bothered her about the bellringer's choice of song clicked in Adele's mind. "Wait — " she said, thinking hard. "Wasn't 'Amazing Grace' written by a former slavetrader to the Americas? How can that be written yet if this is ..."

Adele woke abruptly to find herself on the top bunk in her dorm room.

2

THE GREAT DIVIDE

DURING HER FIRST THREE WEEKS OF COLLEGE, ADELE had found sleep to be a precious commodity. It wasn't just the talkative roommate or the hundreds of pages of assigned reading that kept her from bed, but the effort to introduce herself to every member of the freshman class in hopes of winning a spot on student government. So far, she hadn't found the energy to attend church on Sundays.

But her dream, still vivid in her mind, told her it was time to remedy that. Her efforts at gaining renown were not something God wanted to take backseat to. The rocks and trees might not be crying out their praise in her absence, but certain hunchbacks seemed to be.

Adele squinted at the glowing red digits of her alarm clock, which announced the time as 9:07. If she hurried, she could still make it to a service this morning.

At a quarter past 10, Adele pulled into the parking lot of Glenview Community Church. She was surprised to see a man wearing an orange vest motioning for her to turn left and wondered if perhaps construction were going on. But as she drove past him, she saw dozens of people in orange signaling the rows of traffic to the correct spots. *Parking lot attendants — impressive,* she thought to herself. *Never seen that.*

Inside, it looked like the world's largest family reunion. Adele waded through a sea of people who chatted in groups and sipped at steaming cups of coffee. She picked up a danish from the refreshment table and chewed it absentmindedly as she stared at the information center, filled with attractive brochures detailing all the church's programs. They seemed to have a program for every age and every interest.

Adele followed as the herd began moving toward the sanctuary. Musicians were playing light background music on stage. She found a comfortable seat in the back and settled in.

A man walked up to the mic. "Welcome to Glenview Community Church," he said. "If this is your first time here this morning, we want you to sit back, relax, and enjoy. We're going to start off with a few songs to praise our Lord!" His words were followed immediately by a drum beat as the band transitioned into song.

Adele admired the enthusiasm of the musicians, whose whole bodies seemed caught up in the music, bopping and swaying. The singers' trained voices harmonized perfectly, and they wore expressions of joy. It was great to just watch them praise God.

But as Adele looked around, that's all most people seemed to be doing — watching. A few were clearly belting out the tune, and a fair number were staring at the projected lyrics and mumbling along, but at least half were not singing at all. People seemed to be enjoying themselves, but most were spectators.

The next Sunday, Adele was invited to Good Shepherd Church by Kevin, a freshman who had attended the church his whole life. It was a small traditional church in a small traditional building, shaded by an enormous oak tree nearly as old as the church itself.

They arrived early so Kevin could introduce her to everyone. It was a formal atmosphere, but people were friendly. She met his parents, their neighbors, the pastor, the substitute choir director, and a woman who talked too loudly but which no one seemed to mind. Gradually, Adele noticed there were no other college students around. In fact, while she saw a scattering of younger families, most of the people seemed close to retirement if not well past it.

"So, you must be Kevin's girlfriend," said one of the deacons, shaking her hand and winking at the boy.

"No, sir," Kevin said quickly, calming Adele's sudden fears that perhaps he'd considered this a date. "It's not like that at all. Adele here is just looking for a church that knows something about music."

"Then you are in luck, young lady," the deacon said. "This is a singing church."

And he was right. People were holding the hymnals but she could tell they really didn't need them. At one point, the organ cut out, but the voices carried on in beautiful harmony. Although the sanctuary could have fit 300, the 80 or so attenders filled it to capacity with resonance.

But she noticed Kevin kept his eyes in the hymnal, and sang without much energy. The younger parents, too, sang in a rote manner, as if these songs were someone else's. Adele wondered how much longer this would be a singing church. She could tell the people were holding onto something very dear to them, but it seemed to be a shell of what it was in the past.

"Welcome to Canticle Church. Is this your first time with us?"

"Yes, actually," Adele said.

The greeter gave her a pudgy grin. "Great, we're glad you're here. Do you know much about our church?"

"Not really. I just heard you're a unique church and decided to check it out."

"Well, we welcome you. As it is, you have come on part-singing Sunday." He paused, and Adele gave a quizzical stare. "On part-singing Sunday, our whole church divides into the four major singing parts — melody, alto, tenor and bass."

"O ... K ..." she said hesitantly.

"Since it's your first time, I suggest you sit in the melody section. That's easiest. But who knows — down the road you might be joining any of the sections. You see, at this church we believe music is a powerful language of connecting people, not only to God, but also to each other. We want to help each person grow to full potential in this language. So, once a month, we have part-singing Sunday." He fumbled through the papers in his hand. "Here's a brochure on the whole thing. I think you'll find it quite interesting."

Adele found her way to the melody section and sat down, a tad nervous of what might be asked of her. *I guess John wasn't kidding when he said this church was different.*

She began to thumb through the brochure. The first page read: "We believe God has gifted each person with the ability to give Him praise — and that our praise and worship not only honors God, but lifts up the spirit of the one giving the praise. We believe the ability to offer praise can be improved when worked upon. Though we all have limitations, we all can build upon the innate abilities we have. We want you to be the best with the music of praise that you can be."

Following pages gave more details of how the church made this happen. There was a section on part-singing Sundays, along with a website that could help you learn parts at home. A calendar showed the schedule of workshops on part-singing, learning an instrument, and writing music. Another page gave contact information for church members giving free music lessons for guitar, keyboard, drums, strings, and voice. The back page advertised an upcoming parent-and-teen guitar-making class with testimonials from last year's students.

Adele had never been to a church like this. She wasn't sure what to think — on one hand, she felt like heading for the door, but, on the other, she was intrigued by a church that seemed so interested in what she might be

Praise
THE LORD
with the
LANGUAGE
of
Music.

able to do. They appeared interested in more than just trying to wow people with their own excellence; they actually seemed to care about what an average person like herself might be able to learn and contribute.

In fact, this seemed like the kind of church the bell-ringer was talking about when — *Oh, no. Am I dreaming again? Can a church like this really exist?*

Adele had pinched herself repeatedly during the service but had not woken up. Nor had she wanted to — she'd been enjoying herself far too much. One couple from the church had debuted a new song they'd written called "Mornings with the Savior." Adele stumbled over the words at first, but by the time each part had sung it through separately, she had it half-memorized. When they at last sang as a whole congregation, she was stunned by how caught up she was — perhaps by the beauty of the interwoven voices, or perhaps because she'd let the words become her own prayer to God.

Afterward, Adele had asked the music director, Carl, if she could talk to him. If she were not dreaming, she was curious to know how this place seemed to have sprung from conversations in her mind. Perhaps, years ago, God had given someone else the same dream. Or perhaps God was just preparing her for this morning.

"So, you've just moved here, then?" Carl asked as they sat down in his office.

"Yes. I'm a freshman at State."

"Welcome to the area, then. Have you had a chance

to visit a lot of churches here?"

"So far I've made it to Good Shepherd and Glenview Community, and now here."

Carl smiled. "I see you're browsing from all over the spectrum. Tell me, which style of music did you like better: the contemporary or the traditional?"

"I guess ... I like either. I think I realized this morning that my ability to worship God depends on my attitude — more than on the music style, I mean."

"Flattery will get you nowhere," Carl said, grinning. "But I'm glad to hear it. I spent many years involved in the debate between the old hymns and the new songs before I realized I was fighting the wrong battle."

"How so?"

"Well, most people think the great divide in church music is over style — traditional vs. contemporary. Most worship wars seem to be about these two poles. But they are more alike than you might imagine: They both fail to teach people the language of praise. The great divide is really between churches where only a few people sing and play instruments and churches where everyone is learning to sing and play an instrument, making music part of a daily walk with God."

"Really? Everyone gets involved? I mean — music isn't everyone's thing."

"True. Not everyone is going to get up on stage and do a solo. But that's like saying that reading isn't everyone's thing, so most of us don't have to read the Bible. Song and Scripture are two of the clearest lines of communication we have with God, and yet the temptation is to let those who are more talented than we are speak for us. I'll tell you, Billy Graham is a great speaker, but I'm not going to have him get on the phone and tell my wife how much I love her. I've got to do that myself. Same with music — I'm going to sing to God even if I'm not wonderful at it. Besides, the more I practice singing, the better I'll get, and the more I'll enjoy it."

Adele nodded. "That makes sense. Does it work?"

"You don't motivate people overnight, of course, but over time people have really gotten into it. I think for so many years they didn't know they were allowed to do anything in church except be a spectator. Now, because people are practicing their singing and their music during the week, they can really participate on Sundays. They're looking forward to the service all week because it's where all their practice pays off. They're so excited to be here — it's a night-and-day difference compared with a few years ago."

"So you've been at this for a while."

Carl stared at the ceiling for a moment. "Just under two years, I believe."

"If you don't mind my asking — what happened two years ago?"

Carl chuckled softly. "It actually started with an absurd bet against my father. He's a great proponent of the old hymns, and I was squarely in the contemporary camp at the time, so I bet him I could prove that my style was better than his style. I researched everything I could about music, about American culture, about church mission, and I eventually discovered that we were bickering about the most minuscule differences. To my surprise, I convinced him, too. Once that barrier dropped, he and I began singing together, and I was reminded what music is all about. Our program here at Canticle is just an outgrowth of that enthusiasm for the power of music."

Carl reached over to a small refrigerator and took out a soft drink. He raised his eyebrow at Adele, but she waved away the offer. "I'm confused," she said. "Contemporary music seems worlds away from the old hymns."

"The main difference between contemporary songs and traditional ones is the beat," Carl said, then took a sip of his soda. "Hymns tend to place every word on the downbeat. Here, watch my foot." He began tapping it against the carpet. "There are two strokes to the foot tap. There is the downbeat — when the toe comes down to meet the floor. Then there is the upbeat — when the toe is pointed toward the ceiling. Now, what's a favorite hymn of yours?"

"'Amazing Grace,'" Adele answered before knowing it.

"All right. Now watch my foot as I sing. *A-ma-zing-grace-how-sweet-the-sound.* See, every syllable comes on the downbeat — when my toe hits the floor. Contemporary music, in contrast, puts a lot of the syllables on the upbeat. It is called syncopation. Syncopation is harder to sing. That, in part, explains why older people, those who were raised on the hymns, have a hard time learning the contemporary songs. They are not used to singing on the offbeat. And it also explains why younger people who were not raised on the hymns, but exclusively on contemporary music, think the hymns are kind of boring: because singing every syllable on the downbeat is not as rhythmically complicated — and, in their minds, interesting — as syncopated music."

"That's it? That's the difference?"

"There are the lyrics, too, of course. It's sort of an opposite situation there, because older songs are more complicated in their language — using larger and more ancient words — while the newer songs use the relatively simple phrasing of today. It's funny: I set out to prove that my songs were better because they had more accessible lyrics and more complicated music, and discovered that my father's songs had more accessible music with more complicated lyrics. It was like seeing myself in a funhouse mirror."

Adele smiled. "So if the differences are that small, why is there such a fierce rivalry?"

"I had trouble figuring that out, too." Carl paused to drink again. "But eventually it dawned on me that people don't simply choose a favorite music style, they fall in love with their music. You don't choose your spouse based on a list of pros and cons; you just find this connection to another person that you can't quite explain. People don't understand exactly why music moves them, and they become afraid the magic could slip through their fingers if they don't continue with what they've always done.

"The more people I talk to, the more I'm convinced that the music people love is the style they were listening to during emotion-filled times in their lives. Just hearing music in that same genre will bring these strong emotions back, and move you deeply."

"Because music is sticky," Adele said softly.

"What was that?"

"Just ... well, songs stick to memories, feelings, that sort of thing. Right?"

"Right," Carl said, pleased. "You catch on quickly. It took a little longer to convince my dad, but eventually I showed him how we both loved the style of music we listened to during our teens and twenties, that time in our life when we were becoming men, exploring the world and our place in it — the most emotional parts of our lives. Once we discovered this, we felt free to let go of our desperate grip on our favorite music.

"As long as I knew I could come back to it and get my fix — so to speak — I had no problem exploring my dad's songs. It was much easier to be selfless. Music styles are a lot like foreign languages, I think. For a long time, before either of us spoke a word of each other's language, they created a barrier between us. But once we spoke a little of each other's language, it gave us a patch of common ground. And, I think, we learned to appreciate our own language even more."

"Wow. That's really cool. Does your dad go to this church?"

"No. He lives cross-country. But he's getting his church into the basics of singing, too."

"Really? Is he a music director, too?"

"Nope. Just a ordinary guy eager to help people learn music."

The door opened behind Adele, and a woman stepped in with a stack of papers. Carl excused himself and conferred with the woman for a few minutes.

"So, where were we?" Carl said, as he sat back down.

"You'd explained how your bet with your dad brought you closer to him," Adele said. "But I'm still not sure how that got you both to transform your churches."

Carl took a long drink from his bottle. "In a nutshell, I was inspired by what life was like 50 years ago in America. I really had no idea what the church was like back then, because for most of my life I wouldn't listen to my dad when it came to music. Once we began to sing together, though, I was more open and began to get a picture of what life was like when he was growing up — those emotional times when his favorite music was being set in stone.

"Close your eyes for a moment and try to imagine it: There are no CD players, no tape machines, few record players and radios. If you want music in your life, it usually has to be live. So families sing. They sing on every occasion — ballgames, parties, boys' and girls' clubs, meetings, political rallies, the military. And most people sing in church. And the songs they sing in church they sing over and over. They hum them at work. They gather around the piano at Grandma's house and sing. Not only do people sing, but they play instruments. In the North, every home has a piano. In the South, fiddles and guitars are common. Imagine a family of eight gathered in a circle, singing 'How Great Thou Art,' with Dad, Sis, and Junior playing along on their guitars. My dad always says,

'Music was something you did — not something that was done to you.'"

Adele opened her eyes. "But society has changed, right? I mean, I like the idea of making music as a family, but you can't turn back the clock."

"True, society has changed. Specifically, it began to change in the early '60s with the invention of the transistor radio. That made radios small, and more importantly, cheap. Kids could afford one. They started listening to their own music. Families no longer needed to entertain themselves.

"The church reacted to this change in two primary ways. The traditional churches have kept right on doing what they've always done, ignoring the social shift. But although the church has kept singing its hymns every Sunday, the opportunities to sing those very same hymns during the week became less and less. And before long, the kids with no ties to this old music found it boring and stopped going to church once they grew up.

"So in the early '80s, some churches began using contemporary Christian music to win back these kids. They adapted, taking Christian content and putting it to a beat and note pattern that is closer to what most people currently listen to — on the radio, on television, at the movies, in advertisements. Because the music is closer to what the new people understand, the contemporary church has an easier time of bringing new people in.

"But I believe there is a third, and better, way for churches to respond to this change in society. Because it wasn't just 50 years ago that people sang as part of their daily life; it's been that way for thousands and thousands of years. Music is woven into the very fabric of our being. God created us with this appetite for making music so we might connect ourselves with people and with Him. So I believe that you *can* turn back the clock. I believe that once people get a taste of what it's like to make music, they'll be hungry for it. Rather than ignoring or adapting, I think the church is in the perfect position to take advantage of the social shift and to rejuvenate a nation of spectators.

"Think about it: What if the church were the place that people went to learn music? What if our songs were the ones they practiced every day? What if families started singing again, and the language of music helped bond people like it did with me and my dad — and all the credit went to God?"

Images leaped to Adele's mind from the brochure she'd read this morning. A mother and son writing a song together. A family making a guitar. A bunch of neighbors practicing as a band. "I can see it — the church helping people succeed in their relationships."

"Exactly. We're doing more than telling you how to get close to God and to people; we're helping you."

"That's an exciting mission," Adele said. "But I'm still curious as to how you got your whole church on board for this experiment."

"Well, it actually started pretty small. At the beginning I was just excited to get people interested in music, so I offered a free class on Thursday nights for anyone interested in guitar who'd never actually played. That went so well that I added a class for those who wanted to learn how to sing parts. I added two or three more classes, but it didn't take long before I had stretched myself too thin. So a few of the other musicians in the church started covering for me. Once there were a few of us involved, it became really fun. I was learning a lot, too, because teaching music forced me to really look at it in depth. I got addicted to helping people succeed."

He paused to drink the last of his soda. "It was great. Our church was really changing, not from some program I set up, but because I made a small effort and other people joined me in my enthusiasm. People started doing music as groups and as families, in their devotions and in their spare time. People who thought they were tone-deaf were succeeding at carrying a tune. Suddenly I had this whole pool of people who could sing and play instruments and were willing to help out with the service. It was like I was the coach of a major-league baseball team who suddenly found out that he owned all these minor-league teams where he could find talent. And that he had fans who were playing the sport in their backyard, pumped about going to the big game on Sunday.

"I realized, eventually, that our official music program should support and encourage this movement to put music in people's homes and daily lives. I wrote up a little something ... you know, I might have it around here somewhere." Carl rummaged through drawers. "I wrote up a plan for how our church might get everyone here involved in the effort. Then I took it to our leaders and posed them a challenge. I asked them what criteria they were using to measure the success of our music program. They gave answers like 'the number of people we attract with it,' 'the quality of the music,' and 'that God is praised.'

"Then I suggested that we institute a new measuring stick. I told them our first goal should be to get people singing. I believe my exact statement was, 'We should judge our program by how enthusiastically all the people of the church — especially new people — sing and play their instruments.'"

Carl bent over to look more closely in one of the drawers. "Here it is," he said, pulling out a stack of stapled paper. "I brainstormed a bunch of ideas of how we could encourage music participation on every level — individuals, couples, families, small groups, Sunday service, and even inter-church events. I started out thinking about how it might work in just our church, but I think got carried away and started preaching to the whole world at some point — you'll have to excuse that," he said with a smile. "But if you're interested, you can borrow it."

Adele took the manuscript from him and flipped through the pages. "Sure, that'd be great. Thanks."

"Oh, I think a friend of mine made some notes for me on that copy," Carl said, pointing out some pencil marks. "You can pay as little attention to them as you'd like. Like I said, it was a rough draft, not a blueprint. It ended up as a launching pad for a lot of the things we do here. We let our program take shape based on the people and resources God has given us."

The door opened again, and when Carl saw who it was, he glanced at his watch and stood up hurriedly.

"Seems I've let time get away from me — I'm late for a staff meeting."

Adele stood up to leave. "Oh, I'm sorry. Thanks for talking with me anyway."

"You're welcome. It was very nice to meet you, Adele." He shook her hand, then gestured to the proposal in her other. "You can give that back to me next ... well, are you going to be here next Sunday?"

Adele thought for a moment. "Yes. I imagine I will."

3

MAKING MUSIC PART OF YOUR LIFE

by Carl Reynolds

When I was eight, my dad bought me my first glove. Well, actually, he sold it to me. He felt I'd appreciate it more if I bought it. I paid $2. He showed me how to use it in the backyard. When I was ten, I tried out for Little League. I started in the minors. The next year I joined the *majors*. Though I didn't play much that year, our team won the championship. I still have the trophy: "1967 Little League Champs." In high school I played second base and was a decent player. I thought about going out for the college team, but I decided to pursue other things. Others I knew kept climbing the ladder of baseball success. My roommate's brother went on to play second base for the Cleveland Indians.

I didn't know it at the time, but throughout my school years I was part of the baseball farm team. A farm team is a system of recruitment. The idea is to create opportunities for people to learn an activity with a group of people at a similar skill level. The idea is that you can learn and grow and have a great time competing — and as your skill develops, there is always another team of people with the next level of skill. You go as far as your hard work and innate abilities will take you.

In the end, you have a lot of people that can play and enjoy the activity at some level. And eventually everyone appreciates people at all the different levels. Although I didn't go on to the big leagues, when I watch a baseball game I know how it feels to make a great play, I remember the camaraderie with my teammates and with my dad, and I can follow the strategy and art of the game.

That is what our church needs with music. How do we get every person in church and every new person who walks into church a $2 mitt? Where is the backyard where we can just learn some of the basics? What would the Little League be, where things are a bit more organized, more skills are taught, and there is a joining with others? How do you develop teams where people feel challenged to keep growing in their skill and appreciation for music?

CHAPTER ONE

The game: How individuals can play

The greatest instrument ever made — do you know what it is? Perhaps a Stradivarius violin? A nine-foot Steinway grand piano? Maybe an old Martin D28 guitar? No, the greatest, most complicated, most beautiful, most versatile, most emotional, most unique instrument in the world is one every single person owns — the human voice. And it is free. It was thrown in when you were born. It grows rich with age. It matures with use and practice. And unlike a grand piano that is difficult to take with you backpacking, it goes with you anywhere, anytime. It can be used when you are all alone, or it can join with a friend, or two, or a thousand. How sad it is that we're not making the most of this special gift that God has given us. Most people are watching the "game" of music but are not playing it.

How do you start playing the game? You sing. Sing in the shower. Sing in the car on the way to work (unless you car pool — then get permission). Sing while you work. Sing in church. Sing at parties. Sing at family gatherings. Sing when you mow the lawn, when you

PUSH
OPEN

make dinner, when you take the dog for a walk. The voice is an instrument that must be practiced. If you do not use it, you will lose it.

What will you sing? Perhaps the first songs that jump to mind are favorites you've heard on the radio or from CDs. But the problem is that you can get dependent on the recording. You can sing the song only when you have some form of playback nearby, so you never really learn the song and you never really learn how to sing. If you don't believe me, try this little experiment: Pick a song you have recently fallen in love with on the radio and try singing without the recording. Unless you are really good at music, my guess is it will not go well.

The best way to sing is to sing songs you know. But here is a problem. Many do not really know that many songs. Oh, we know a phrase here and there — maybe a verse or two if we don't get them mixed up. But how many songs, from beginning to end, do you know by heart? You see, the songs we know by heart are the ones we are going to sing in the shower, on a morning walk, and on any occasion that song comes upon us.

So my suggestion is to decide to really learn a few songs by heart, from top to bottom. Why not start with ten? And why not memorize five traditional hymns and five contemporary songs? If you like only traditional songs, this will be a good exercise in broadening your horizons. If you like only contemporary, this will be more helpful than you think — traditional songs are easier to sing without an instrument keeping the beat. I guarantee that if you memorize ten songs, you will automatically find yourself singing these songs sometime throughout your day without even thinking about it.

"OK," you say, "but what if I can't sing?" Well, how do you know that you can't sing? Enjoying singing does not depend on the quality of your voice. Your voice is not bad; it just has character. In fact, the neat thing about music is that when you take a hundred lousy voices and put them together, it sounds like a pretty good choir.

"But," you counter, "my problem isn't the quality of my voice; it is a problem with pitch. I just can't stay on pitch." Personally, I believe a lot of people have this problem because they are so dependent on singing with recordings or with other people. The best way to sharpen your skills is to sing, not only with other people, but also on your own. And to sing often.

"You don't understand," you say. "I'm flat-out tone deaf." Let me tell you something: There are very few really tone-deaf people, and you are probably not one of them. If you're a male, let me try to explain what may have happened to you. When we men are boys, we sing like girls — with a high voice. But about age 13, our voices start heading south. And when that happens, many guys lose their way. Technically speaking, what happens is boys are singing in the same octave as girls. But when their voices have fully changed, they are singing one octave lower than the girls. In the middle of the change some boys can't figure out which octave they should be singing in, so they start singing as low as they can. Soon that is all they sing — a few notes down low — and they get labeled monotone (literally: one tone). After a few years, it gets ingrained, and we declare them tone deaf.

It doesn't have to stay this way. Any music teacher could help. In fact, any person who knows how to sing at all may be able to help. For most people, all it takes is some education about octaves and scales, and then regular practice. Learning to carry a tune is a simple matter of effort, not talent.

So now you've memorized your ten songs and you are singing them at every chance. What's next? Why not learn harmony? Harmony adds depth and richness to the total experience of music — both in hearing it and in doing it. Harmony helps you experience music at many levels, and it also helps you experience other people in a fun and exciting way. Because harmony needs other voices.

Learning harmony might sound scary or confusing, but it is a really simple concept: The main part of a song is called the melody. This is the tune everyone is familiar with. Harmony is simply another song that goes alongside it, either a few notes higher or a few notes lower than the main part. When you put the two songs together, you get a much richer sound. Harmony and the melody are, together, more than the parts. Something new is created.

New learners of harmony can get discouraged because they often lose the harmony part and start singing the melody. You have to remember that the melody is the most natural part to sing, and most likely you have burned those notes into your memory. It will take time to burn in the harmony part. But trust me — it will happen. And once it does, the next song you try to learn the harmony for will be easier.

Now, all this may sound somewhat complicated. Music can be. But it doesn't have to be. Most people can go a lot further with singing than they would ever dare to believe. I have seen it over and over. So, at the very least, ask someone who seems more musical than you to mentor you a bit. Or join a choir. Or take music lessons — any money you spend will be well worth it.

We have been given this extraordinary instrument — the human voice — and it is a total waste not to develop it for our own pleasure, for others' pleasure, and most importantly, for God's pleasure. And without working on it — without playing the game on our own — all we are doing is winging it every Sunday in church.

The human voice is our greatest instrument, but let me make a case for learning a conventional instrument as well. First of all, it's fun. It really is. And second, it is magical.

I remember being excited going into fourth grade: We were going to be introduced to our first instrument — the recorder. First the teacher taught us individual notes on our plastic flutes. I couldn't see how that would become music. How could individual notes put together make a continuous seamless stream? But it did. I was making music on a piece of plastic with holes.

Not only are instruments fun and magical, but they support your singing. First, an instrument added to your voice makes a bigger, fuller sound. The guitar strings or piano strings are actually adding harmony to the melody of your voice. It's something like being the lead singer in a choir. Second, an instrument makes singing contemporary songs easier. In traditional music, the syllables come primarily on the downbeat, whereas in contemporary music they often come on the offbeat. You can succeed at singing hymns without an instrument because you can measure the downbeats quite easily in your head. But contemporary music is hard to sing without an instrument keeping a strong beat. That is its weakness; that is its strength. Because it works a lot better with instruments, contemporary music forces more people of the congregation to learn an instrument. And if you want music to happen at church and in every church member's home, someone in each family will have to learn an instrument. That is exactly what we want.

Which instrument should you learn? Any instrument you choose is a great choice. But for accompanying singing, I would recommend piano and guitar. Most instruments, like trumpet or flute, cannot be played while singing. Second, most instruments can play only one note at a time. If you are the only one playing, you tend to play the melody. The melody is what you sing. So there is no choir effect. With the piano and guitar, you can play and sing at the same time. Both also are capable of playing more than one note at the same time, thus are great for the choir effect.

The piano is one of the greatest instruments ever invented. When it came into being, it threatened to put the symphony out of business because it could imitate the whole symphony. One drawback, however, is that it takes a lot of practice and time before you are able to accompany singing. But the effort and time are definitely worth it.

The guitar is probably the other great instrument. It is one of the easiest instruments to learn the basics of, so you can start to play and sing very quickly. If you were to learn just three chords (three different patterns of strings you push down with your fingers), I could teach you how to play 100 songs. Contemporary songs suit the guitar very well.

Is this true?

If you want to learn the piano, take lessons. If you want to learn the guitar, take lessons, or find someone who plays and ask for help getting started. With very little guidance, you can be playing and singing in a month. The only thing standing in the way of you and music is a little effort. Just remember that the more you put into music, the more you'll get out of it.

Aren't you being a bit too optimistic?

CHAPTER TWO

The backyard: How couples and families can play

Baseball has lost some of its luster since the days it was considered the national pastime. Some people blame the big star salaries and even bigger egos. Some people blame the growth of distractions like TV, malls, or the internet. While these certainly play a part, the main reason baseball has suffered is because parents and kids don't play catch in the backyard the way they used to. Families are no longer the center of the baseball world.

The trend now is to let the organized part of the baseball world do the training. Send your kid to Little League. Have him go out for the school team. But the power of baseball is not the game itself. The power of baseball is its ability to connect people to each other. The game is the excuse to come together.

Now, as a parent you might not be the best baseball teacher, and consequently your kid may not be learning the greatest baseball technique, but he will be connecting with you. That is what the game in the backyard, the game in your home, does — it connects your family to each other. Today, baseball unites only baseball fans, but 50 years ago it united families, neighborhoods, communities — the country. That's the power of the backyard.

The same might be said about music: You could send your kids to school where they learn an instrument in band. Your child learns an instrument, but whom does he connect with? His band teacher and band mates. And what happens when he graduates? The instrument more than likely goes into a closet never to be played again — after graduation, the venue for playing it is gone. The advantage of the family venue is it lasts a lifetime.

Family is where you live most of the time. The day-in, day-out activities you do as a family might not seem special when taken individually, but as a whole they have great power to shape and influence you. Yet we are losing all these little habits that help define us. We no longer play baseball together; we drive the kids around to four or five different sports. We no longer make music together; we each get our own headphones to listen to our own favorite style. Sadly, music is probably the number-one item today that separates family members from each other.

Maybe not #1 - but definitely a problem

That is the danger of recorded music vs. live. Recorded music allows us each to escape into our own isolated world. With live music you need to come together to make it happen.

Instead of driving a wedge between family members, music could unite you as you work to create something that none of you could create on your own. If you make your home the venue for playing music, for praising God, then those habits have a good chance of sticking for life. Music could become your family pastime.

Before you involve the kids — or if you are married and have no kids — you'll want to create a habit of music-making in your marriage. Any couple knows that your spouse is the closest living human being for you on the planet. Music is one of the most powerful connectors and memory-builders that there is. It is one of our chief means of praising God. And yet it goes unused, untapped in the average Christian marriage. How can this be?

Couples have a great advantage in learning music, because two people learning something together have a greater chance of success than one. Take the steps you learned in the last chapter — sing, learn harmony, learn an instrument — and do them together. Ecclesiastes 4:9-10 reminds us, "Two are better than one, because they have a good return for their work: If one falls down, his friend can help him up."

Though the potential for success is greater with two, there are some major obstacles to overcome. For instance, if you've never sung with your spouse, sitting down at the kitchen table and singing a hymn together might be a bit awkward. It's funny that we can be so self-conscious with the person we are the most intimate with. There's the fear of trying something new, for starters, but mostly it's uncomfortable because exposing your voice is so personal. But so is sleeping in the same bed. Somehow, married couples get over that embarrassment — through much repetition — and the same thing will happen with singing together.

Start out singing in the car with a tape. Then move to the house. Finally, try it tape-free. With a little practice, it will be no problem. Make it part of your marriage devotions.

Remember, music is a powerful connecting force. Find a special song to mark your anniversary. Sing it together every year. When your children celebrate your 50th anniversary, and you (or they) sing your anniversary song, there will not be a dry eye in the place.

If one of you plays an instrument, this music thing together should be no problem. If neither of you plays, why not both learn? Take lessons together. It will give you an excuse to be together — an excuse that could last the rest of your days together.

The nurses, the doctors, and visitors were drawn to the room at the end of the hall. They said it was because of the love emanating from it. My wife's best friend's parents were both dying in the hospital at the same time. And as their eight sons and daughters kept vigil over their last week on the earth, they sang. They sang songs they learned as children. They sang songs their parents had a lifetime of memories with. They sang songs they had sung together in church. But it wasn't the music that attracted the nurses, the doctors, and visitors to the room at the end of the hall. It was the love. That's what they said: "You can feel the love in that room." The music was just the means to express it.

That is what music does. It connects us, it communicates for us, and it joins us in emotional ways that would otherwise be awkward for most families. It allows us to say things to each other and God that we wouldn't otherwise have the emotional courage to say. It allows us to connect with our shared past without someone retelling all the shared past. It allows us to feel emotion at a level we might otherwise run away from.

If you want love emanating from your hospital room one day, start laying the groundwork now. Begin while the kids are young. Kids love to sing. They will sing regardless of whether you encourage them or not. They will sing whatever they listen to. They are sponges soaking up their environment. And they are not fussy about what they pick up. They will pick up songs from TV shows and commercials, from tapes and CDs, from what you the parents listen to, from what older brothers and sisters listen to.

Kids like songs because songs are repeatable. Kids like repeatable things. They will watch the same video over and over — I'm sure I've seen "Dumbo" a thousand times with my four boys. Children are looking for things they recognize, because they are trying to make sense of the world, and so love repeated things. Songs fit the bill perfectly — they are made to be sung again and again.

If you want the music you teach your children to last a lifetime, it's important to attach particular songs to certain events. Take a look at Christmas music. It seems that every popular artist in the world has a Christmas album. Why is their popularity so strong? Because Christmas songs are sung only once a year and mark a very specific occasion. As the years go by, the memories that get attached to these songs get stronger and stronger. There is nothing magical about Christmas songs. You can make the same thing happen with other events and other songs.

Attach songs to daily events: Pick out a bedtime song for each of your kids. Sing at the table — have a prayer and a song at every meal. When our kids were young, we had each child pick out a song he wanted us to sing. They still remember those songs fifteen years later. Sing before you begin your family devotions each day. Look at the daily habits your family already has and pick something that works best for you.

Attach songs to weekly events: Pick a song for your kids to sing when they get out of school for the weekend. Sing a certain song each week before church as preparation for worship. Singing during weekly chores can help lift some of the drudgery. Use your imagination.

Attach songs to monthly events: Try starting a monthly family talent show where everyone tries to do something with music. Celebrate the start of a new month with a song. Call your relatives once a month and sing a song about family on that day.

Attach songs to yearly events: Find a special song for the birth of each of your children. Have the congregation at your church sing it at the baptism. Sing that song on their birthday every year. That song will be special the rest of

their lives — and yours.

Choose a song to mark your yearly vacation. Before you head out the driveway, have a family prayer and sing the family vacation or camping song. If you get together with other families for camping, have everyone sing it around a campfire.

Holidays are simple to attach a song to because they are already on your calendar. Make a New Year's Eve song part of your family tradition on the last day of the year. Sing it every year. For Easter, make the dough for hot cross buns the night before — the crosses represent Christ's crucifixion. First thing on Easter Sunday, put the buns in the oven, read the resurrection story in Luke 24, and sing "Christ the Lord is Risen Today."

Christmas already has so many songs attached to it that you might feel you don't need to add anything. But what singing event is specifically related to your family? One day you will want your kids to come home for Christmas, but what special things will they come home for? Why not, on every Christmas Eve, light candles in a dark family room, read Luke 2, and sing "Silent Night"? Simple, easy, and any family can do it. Repeat this Christmas Eve event every year and watch your kids flock home for Christmas Eve when they are older, bringing with them friends, boy- and girlfriends, spouses, and kids. They'll want to share it with others.

Attach songs to one-time events: Mark significant changes in your family's life with a song. If you move, get a new job, or go to a new church, choose a song of celebration — or if it has you worrying, a song about trusting God and surrendering your fears.

You see what we are trying to do here: create powerful bonds that connect memories and people and God. The collective layering of memories creates powerful relationship emotions. Music — and everything dealing with music — is an effective way to make this happen. Be creative: One unconventional approach I used was making a guitar. My son and I bought a guitar kit, which includes all the wood and parts needed to put it together. It was quite a challenge — I am not Mr. Woodworking. But I went on the internet and downloaded all sorts of instructions and pictures from people who'd done this before. When we finally completed it, we began using the guitar in our family worship times. When my son leaves home, the guitar — with all his memories of worship, family, and dad — will go with him. Twenty years later, if his house were burning down, that memory-laden guitar would be the first thing he grabs.

In many ways, the music game in the backyard is the hardest to get going and to maintain. You will probably run into a few brick walls before you can succeed. But keep going — it is also the most rewarding.

understatement!

The first major wall to family music is parents who do not sing or play instruments and think it is because they are not gifted in it. If this is you, read the last chapter again. Besides, you do not have to be gifted in music to do family music. Even if you are one of the very few human beings who cannot sing no matter what, you can still create an environment for singing in your home. You just have to get things going; your kids will supply what you lack.

The second potential wall is thinking that you've already blown it because your kids are too old. But it doesn't matter. They may be 3, 10, 17, 30, or 45 years old — it is never too late to start playing the church-music game in your backyard. So your daughter is 30 and you failed to pick a hymn or contemporary Christian song to mark her birth — pick one out now. At the next family gathering, present it to her. Sing it with her on every succeeding birthday. If there is a great distance between you, sing it to her over the phone. It is never too late. Do something. Play. Sing. It is possible.

The third big wall is that your kids become

teenagers. Music is easy when kids are younger. They love you; they love what you love. They freely express themselves with no worry as to how they sound. When they get older, they start developing a love for music that is different from yours — and many times, it's music you cannot stand. They become more self-conscious, and suddenly family singing isn't what it used to be.

Never give up

Don't give up. Keep singing your annual songs; even if your kids appear uninterested on the outside, they'll still recognize your interest. For some of your other traditions, maybe it's time to let them pick the song. Give them some ownership of the process, and learn something about their interests. But most important, involve some other people their age, getting together to make music with other families and groups. You want to expand your game beyond the backyard and into the sandlot.

CHAPTER THREE

The sandlot: How informal groups can play

The game of baseball in the backyard is fun — for a while. But soon a family tires of it. There aren't enough players to make a really good game. It's hard to improve when you're playing with the same small group of people. There's nothing to work hard for. That is why the game usually drifts over to the sandlot. All the kids who were playing ball in the backyard now come together in a sandlot and have a more spirited, competitive game.

Music needs the same thing. You need the support and the opportunity to grow that the sandlot gives you. The sandlot is any venue for playing and singing that goes beyond your family but is not yet organized and formal. Everyone is allowed to play on the sandlot, and no one sits on the bench.

Extended-family gatherings are a great excuse for singing and playing — birthday parties, baptisms, marriages, Christmas parties, etc. Cousins could bring their instruments and show Grandma and Grandpa how they are coming along. A family hymn-sing could ensue.

The extended-family music time gives your

own family a venue to practice for. Cousins may be competing to keep up with each other on their guitar lessons. At the same time, a rich extended-family singing tradition is being developed — a tradition that will pay off in the future during large family celebrations and crisis times.

Sometimes your extended family is not open to these kinds of things. Maybe half the family members are not Christian, or are just into other things, or live so far away that you rarely get together. Then make use of surrogate extended families. These are families nearby who have a family situation like you and also have the same interest in developing music in their families as you.

Once a month, get together with a few families for music. Have an instrument recital. Sing songs. In the summer, do it around the campfire. In the winter, go skiing together and gather in the evenings to sing the songs you have learned by heart over the last year.

Learn from each other. I play the guitar — in fact, I own four of them — and have never paid for lessons. In 1978 I went on a summer mission program that landed me in the middle of nowhere in Nicaragua. Bill Green was my partner, and we each bought a $10 guitar from the market. Every day we tried to play the guitar. Every day we got a little better. Then, while at seminary in 1980, I started hanging out with Harley Faber, who taught me how to lead singing with the guitar. We played together. Our wives soon joined us, and we formed a band.

Make little bands of all ages and abilities in the sandlot. Being around musicians at your level will keep you from getting either too bored or too discouraged. Bands are fun, they're great for learning music, and they'll connect you to your relatives and neighbors. Most importantly, a band practices not only for its own enjoyment but to eventually play in front of people. And that's the direction we're heading: out of the sandlot and into little league.

CHAPTER FOUR

The little league: How church groups can play

Playing ball in the backyard is fun. Playing ball in the sandlot is exciting. But the better you get at the sport, the more you'll desire to play at a bigger, more organized venue. I remember putting on my first Little League uniform. When I looked in the mirror, I saw a baseball player looking back.

This is where the church is uniquely placed in all of society to create such venues. Of course, it has the weekly church service. But for most this is too much of a talent leap. Most are not ready for the major leagues. So why not create the minor leagues?

Most churches used to provide opportunities for minor-league play with monthly hymn sings. Because it was not the Sunday worship service, there was a certain informal freedom to try things — new songs, new instruments. It was an opportunity for people to come forward and do things they would not feel comfortable doing in the worship service. But this venue for music has all but disappeared. People are not playing the music game in their backyards or sandlots, so the love of the game has dwindled. When churches try to do a little-league event, no one comes.

But if there are strong backyard and sand-lots in the church, a "praise sing" can become a popular field for all this musical energy to go to the next level. Families working on songs could come up and sing and play. Informal bands could take turns leading some of the songs. And because this is the little league, the quality does not have to be perfect. A band of seventh graders learning the guitar could come up. A trio of third graders. A quartet of guys who are taking voice lessons.

What if the church had talent night twice a year? Think of the fun and excitement. When my wife and I spent time as missionaries in the Philippines in the early '80s, some of my fond-est experiences were the talent nights. I was amazed at what average people ended up doing. Music was often a part of it. The genius of the little league is that it gives motivation for average people to play the game in their life. If there is no place to bring one's talent, then no one works at it.

All the small groups of the church can be possible little-league venues. The youth group can be a showcase for all the youth who are learning various instruments, singing, and har-mony. The youth could make use of music at every meeting. There could be various member

bands that lead the music at the youth meetings. The groups could do their own talent nights. They could do a mid-year "praise carol" (like a Christmas carol) where they visit some of the older folks of the community and sing some of the old songs outside their door. They could have singing evangelistic groups in the park. Any of the groups in the church could do the same — young couples, MOPS, Bible study groups, Sunday school, even the nursery.

The church could sponsor a song-writing contest. When my wife and I arrived on Negros Island in the Philippines, we were surprised that our mission was teaching English church songs to the people in the villages. We were told it was because the people liked to sing English. But we quickly learned they liked to sing English for prestige's sake; it was not the language of their heart. We decided our students should sing in their own language, but the problem was that there were no church songs in their language. So we sponsored a song-writing contest among the 40 or so students. The songs they wrote were so great we put them in a book, and some of those same songs are still being sung 18 years later.

If the church holds such a contest every year, we'll be just as amazed at what comes out of it — individuals, families, and groups of people working in creative and unique ways to produce praise music that will not only honor God but bring our people closer together. One contest could be for writing special songs to mark special events in our church's history — events that will be remembered year after year with the singing of the song.

The church could hold a music honors ceremony. Philippians 3:17 says to "join with others in following my example, brothers, and take note of those who live according to the pattern we gave you." Often missed here are the key words "take note." If you want people to grow in a certain area, you have to take note of their progress. We do this in all areas of life — with grades, with promotions, with trophies, with awards and plaques. If we want people to succeed and grow in the music game, we need to find ways to let people know that they are on the right track and progressing forward. Honor all the people learning to sing. Have a "show and tell" for those crafting their own instruments. Get creative in what and whom you recognize. Let the church be the one giving out a certificate honoring them for their progress.

The little league is so important. It's at this level the church leadership has to step to the plate to make things happen. The harder the church works at the minor leagues, the more skilled people will be to participate in the major leagues — the church service.

CHAPTER FIVE

The major league: How the church can play

Two dollars were burning a hole in my pocket. I was out with the guys, on a long bus ride. I tingled with the anticipation ... the wonder ... the excitement. It was 1967, and our destination was Tiger Stadium, home of the soon-to-be world champion Detroit Tigers. The Little League team I had played for was on a field trip.

I had never been to a professional game. I soaked in the atmosphere of the stadium: the feel of the hard benches. The smell of hot dogs and stale pop. The sounds of laughter and excitement all around. And finally a sight I had never seen before — thousands of people, young and old — a crowd so large they looked like ants making their way up and down the bleachers.

It was a strange feeling. This baseball field was like our baseball field. This baseball team was like our baseball team. This game that was about to be played was the same game we Little Leaguers played. But it was different, too. It was bigger. It was brighter. And it was definitely louder.

The players finally came out. The crowd cheered. We did, too. We were a part of the crowd. Even though we did not know a fraction of those gathered there in historic Tiger Stadium, we all felt part of each other. We didn't need to know much about the people in the crowd. It was enough that they loved the same thing we did.

Not only were we connected in our love for the game, we also felt like our contribution made a difference. If we cheered loudly and with more heart, somehow good things happened. And what umpire could possibly get things right without a little help from thousands of distant eyes that could see clearly when it came to who was safe and who was out?

Not only did we influence the players as they battled on the field, we became the players. When a Tiger got a hit, we all got a hit. When Mickey Stanley slid into second base, we all slid into second base ... headfirst. When Willie Horton hit a home run, we all trotted around the bases to the cheers of adoring fans.

For three hours, the players, the crowd, and I were one. When it was over, we got in the bus and headed for home.

Where is the stadium experience for those playing the game of music? Where can they sit down with a big crowd and join a group of talented players and feel like they are one? Where can the excitement of big-league play energize them for their daily practice? The church service, of course.

In most churches, the Sunday service is the focus of the music program's energy and resources — but in the farm-team system, the service is just the end product of the behind-the-scenes efforts of the music program. The service is just the final expression of all the effort and enjoyment that has been going on all during the week.

In the church service, all the levels get to play the game. Everyone is brought together. Those who have been learning on their own all week get to experience their music on a bigger scale — when I'm tapping my foot, it's reinforced by the bass drum. When I'm singing the notes, hundreds of others singing along makes for a richer, fuller sound. Even if I'm a little off, I'm still contributing to the overall effect, because without slight variances in pitch, a choir would sound like just one person singing. In the service, there's an energy and excitement in the singing, and a sense of coming together and belonging.

For those who have been learning to play in families, small groups, and bands, the service can be a place to honor their efforts. A family could sing "Silent Night" while lighting one of the Advent candles. The winner of the song-writing contest could perform the song for the whole congregation. From time to time, you could even have Guitar Sunday, where everyone who can play just three chords gets up and leads simple songs. Have an annual Youth Service, Senior Service, or Moms Service. Giving others a small taste of what it's like on the playing field might motivate them to someday join the big leagues.

For those who will be leading the music, this level is a reward for their hard work and diligence in practicing. It becomes a level in the music program to work toward: Only the best get to lead at the service. At first, this might seem inconsistent with the general philosophy of getting as many people into music as possible. Why not let everyone who is willing participate? But, remember, you don't get to step up to the plate at a major-league baseball game just because you are willing. Nor do we let everyone who is willing to preach give a sermon. There are some smaller steps that lead up to preaching or directing the music in front of the whole congregation. It's not that you don't get to play, but you have to play at your own level. If we do away with the levels, then we discourage people from growing in that particular area. If you practice guitar an hour a day, and I practice an hour a month, and we both get to lead in the church service, then you will soon become unmotivated because there is no reward for your hard work.

The reward of playing in the service must not be based solely on one's skill, though — sometimes people end up leading music because of their innate talent, but they do not really have a walk with God. Reward people for their ability to worship God with music and to help others worship God with music. The prestige of major-league play can be used to encourage growing with God as well as in music.

The other important goal of the Sunday service is to help those who are not playing the music game to get involved. It is a chance to advertise the joy of learning music and making it part of daily life. It is a place to give people the tools and motivation to succeed in the backyard. You could teach some aspects of singing right there in the service by having a Part-Singing Sunday where the congregation divides up into the four parts and each is taught, one group at a time, how to sing a particular song before joining again to form a choir. You could encourage people to memorize songs by choosing a Song of the Month, singing it every Sunday, and handing out the lyrics for people to practice, then on the last

Sunday of the month singing it from memory.

The ultimate goal of church is to bring together human beings and God. Music is a tool we use to help cement that connection. Use the same patterns we learned in the backyard for keeping families connected: Repeat songs, and tie them to certain events. Try establishing traditions for important times of the church year: Christmas, Lent, Easter, Old Testament festivals, Thanksgiving, etc. Remember that most people who are getting started in music are going to need a lot of repetition before a song sinks in, so make lyrics and tapes available, and don't be afraid to sing a song several weeks in a row. That makes it a together project. Nothing contributes to church unity like one member helping another get close to God.

CHAPTER SIX

The world series: How many churches can play

We are not a league unto ourselves. Each church does not have to try to do this music thing alone. We are part of the largest organization in the world today. There are more Christians belonging to the church than any other people belonging to any other body. And music is the language of praise for all of them. Yet we often go it alone.

Easy to forget this

What if churches from all over the world were getting people to use music in their lives? What if there were online forums and chat rooms where people could connect with others who are trying to teach harmony to their children in their home? What if there were Christian guitar-making guilds that consisted of interested church members around the globe? What if there were a club of Christian songwriters who could share songs they'd written for their churches with every other church on the planet? What if denominations had gatherings in stadiums, where thousands of people of diverse backgrounds could come to praise God in song?

You are a big dreamer, Carl!

The first steps toward these dreams will be

1st Annual
BATTLE
OF THE

small. Begin with a Christian songwriting contest just among the churches in a small city or township. Or organize a "battle of the church bands" in your area. Or rent out the town stadium (which may be the high school) and have a Guitar Sunday with 1,000 guitars leading the service. If even these are too hard to organize, get together with a sister church to work on these ideas.

It is easy to get caught up in our small communities and programs and miss the big picture of what God has in store for the church. Ephesians 4:4 (NLT) reminds us, "We are all one body, we have the same Spirit, and we have all been called to the same glorious future." When we join together, our churches become stronger, "so that the whole body is healthy and growing and full of love." (verse 16).

Before we get too enthusiastic, though, it's important we remember not to start out with one of these big events. Churches have tried such efforts in the past with little success. They do not work because we do not have churches filled with players. Spectators, when given another opportunity to go to another big event, can take it or leave it. Players, when given an opportunity to go to a large event where they can interact with other talented players, jump at the chance.

It all depends on the backyard. If music is

not happening in the backyard, then the farm-team system breaks down, and soon it isn't happening anywhere. The big leagues and the championships might get the most notice, but the key to the long-term success of the sport lies in the backyard: the music game in people's homes. We judge our success by how enthusiastically all the people of the church — especially new people — sing and play their instruments.

CHAPTER SEVEN

The $2 mitt: How to get newcomers to play

Music is the language of the world. It is a memory catcher. It captures and communicates peoples' hopes and dreams, their joy and sorrow, their passion, their fear, their struggle, their memories, their brokenness and pain, their faith, their desires and wants. It is a powerful emotional force. It connects in a way nothing else does. It speaks messages, it warms cold hearts, and it finds its way past well-placed barriers to the soul.

Yet most people are content to sit and watch. They buy their CDs and tune into MTV. It is not because they aren't skilled enough to make music. It is because no one ever gave them a $2 mitt and tossed the ball with them.

The church spends millions of dollars and work hours each year trying to reach the unchurched, and yet most churches, far from taking advantage of the fact that almost every human being can relate to music and is interested in it, do very little with new people and music. Instead of harnessing the power of music, we often let it be a stumbling block. A new person walks in. Songs are sung she has never heard before. The words, the beat, the pitch patterns are such that she has no emotional memory bank that she can relate them to, so from her point of view they feel flat. The church people don't see this, because their emotional banks are filled with these kinds of songs, and they think that everyone should be as moved as they are. If the new person keeps coming, no one helps her get up to speed. She is on her own.

Why not get the songs to the new people before they come to church? Put some of the songs on tape. Have people over to learn and enjoy the songs. Create memories with them. When they finally come to your service, they will know the songs already. They will get a rush of emotions, finally singing songs they know with a group. All the energy of the past will meet the new energy of the moment, and something may happen at a deeper level.

You mean use secular songs and redeem them?

Or use songs that tap into their past: Churches could have a '50s music service, or '60s, or '70s — who wouldn't be interested in hearing how God relates to their particular taste in music? In every era there are songs about looking for answers, seeking God, or awe of the created world. Sing these songs and show how they point toward fulfillment in relationship with God. Newcomers have twenty, thirty, or forty years of layers of memories with these songs but probably never considered the deeper meanings beneath the surface.

What if church were the place you went if you wanted to learn music? Already, church is the only venue where average people can go on a regular basis and participate in music. Let's take advantage of this fact. Let's make it a place where they can find free lessons, connections to other musicians, regular practice, and weekly musical inspiration. Let them come for the music first and get to know God in the process. Let them see that you are interested not in just entertaining them, not just trying to impress them, but wanting to help them impress themselves with their own growth. Tossing the ball with them is just one way to show, like my father showed me, that we love them.

Music is the connecting language of the soul.

Remember, the power of music is not the game itself but its ability to connect people to each other. It's an excuse to come together. If we do not come together with those who don't know Christ, if we instead hold up music as a barrier between us, then all our gifts and time and labor are wasted. "If I have the gift of prophecy and can fathom all mysteries and all knowledge," says Paul in 1 Corinthians 13:2, "but have not love, I am nothing."

4

THE NEW CITY

CURLED UP IN A CHAIR, HUDDLED NEAR THE ONLY light her roommate would let her have on at two in the morning, Adele finished reading the last chapter of Carl's treatise on music.

She was tired, but her mind seemed awake to the possibilities. She jotted down some ideas of places she might find an inexpensive guitar, and a few of her favorite songs that she wanted to memorize. She let herself imagine playing at a campus coffeehouse with some of her friends. It was almost like she was there — bright lights, the rush of adrenaline, people watching. Before she knew it, she had closed her eyes, and fallen to sleep.

It seemed impossibly dark in the small room. A small glint of metal was all she could see, and yet her surroundings seemed familiar. The faint smell of damp wood, and the sound of wind whistling between planks, reminded her of somewhere she'd been before.

"You have another question, perhaps?" a baritone voice said out of the darkness. She smiled, recognizing

the familiar voice.

"No," she answered, "just a thank you."

She felt a strong hand grab her small one and lead her downstairs, out of the belltower. Outside, on the walkway between the towers, she could finally see the bellringer in the moonlight. She looked warmly at him, hesitating to speak for fear the moment would whisk away.

At last she managed to find her voice. "I want to thank you for all your advice," she told him. "I'm taking up an instrument."

"Not the bells, I assume," he said, giving her a lopsided smile.

"No," she laughed. "It's hard to start a band with those."

Again they fell into silence. Words seemed secondary to just being there. Together, they stood on the walkway and looked over the whole of Paris. The shapes of buildings were difficult to make out, but stretching into the distance were thousands of lights flickering — candles in windows, lanterns in the hands of passersby. The city seemed both invisible and alive.

"This is my favorite time of day," the bellringer said. The wind rustled his hair. "It's moments like this that I can almost see the new city."

"The new city?"

"You're just one person, right? You can learn music, and you can praise God, and that's just like a light in God's eyes. Maybe you get a few friends together and make a band. That's a few lights. Maybe you even get your whole church to really sing for God, and that's a few hundred lights. But in your whole life, you're never going to see the whole picture. You're never going to see the millions and millions of lights all together, so many that your eyes can't see the end of them. That's what I think we'll find, at last, in the City of Heaven."

He stretched out his arm and pointed into the distance. "Can't you picture it? Can't you feel the immensity of the crowd? Can't you feel it — so close — just beyond?"

She strained to see as he did, for even a glimpse of it.

"That's what keeps me going up here, when I sometimes wonder why I bother at all with music. Time will pass, and my life will end, but I will still be singing. I'm just rehearsing right now for a concert beyond what I can even imagine."

With that, she began to hear the faint sounds of song. Every flame was a voice, every voice a soul of praise. "Amazing grace," the voices sang, "how sweet the sound, that saved a wretch like me." Adele's heart welled with emotion, feeling the words go straight to God's ears. "I once was lost, but now am found, was blind — but now I see."

"And, lo, a great multitude, which no
man could number, of all nations, and
kindreds, and people, and tongues, stood
before the throne, and before the Lamb ...
and cried with a loud voice, saying,
'Salvation to our God which sitteth upon
the throne, and unto the Lamb.'"

— *Revelation 7:9-10, KJV*

POSTSCRIPT

This book was designed to get you excited about music, and the possibilities it has for the church. It's tried to give you a goal to pursue and a lot of ideas of how to get there. But the most intricate playbook — to borrow Carl's metaphor — can't get the ball game going. It takes someone taking a chance and saying, "Let's do this." And then it takes some prodding and pushing and cheerleading — it takes leadership. At every level it takes someone willing to say, "Play ball."

If you are just an average person in an average church, you might feel powerless to start a revolution in church music. But you can start playing the game yourself. If you can't carry a tune, get help. Don't buy into the lie that you were just born a non-singer. If you can sing melody, learn harmony. Join the church choir. Then take up an instrument. Do whatever it takes to grow in music. If help costs money, spend it. Music is the language of the heart.

If you're married, involve your spouse in the learning. If you have children, no matter how young or old your children are, do something with music. Have a family worship service once a week. Memorize one song a month. Practice in the car on the way to ballgames and other family activities. Let music be something that brings your family together.

Then find another family with kids close to your kids' ages who want to do the same thing in their family. They'll see how much fun you're having, and want to join in. Then you can support each other and schedule joint times of music — playing instruments and singing together.

Add another family or two. Offer to share in front of the church how music has changed your life with God. More people will want to join in with you. The music director will see all this budding talent and want to know how he can support the learning. The singing in the service will take on a new sheen. New people will be attracted, and other churches will look to yours as an example, and the kingdom of God will grow. Why? Because families will be worshipping God all through the week. Miracles start happening when God's people are filled with worship.

Perhaps you have some level of leadership at your church. You already know something about music. Then you have even more resources at hand to change the way your church does music.

If you're a small-group leader, teach your group how to sing and play an instrument with worship songs. If it goes well, have the members move practice into their families and neighborhoods. Talk to other small-group leaders about your success and help them get music going in their own groups.

If you're a member of the choir or play an instrument on the music team, you might not be able to change the whole music program. But you can offer free lessons to a friend. You can write a new song for your church to sing. You can suggest and help organize a talent night. You can start a band with others on your team. You can gather some friends for praise caroling.

If you are the music coordinator of your church, you have a more direct means of getting your on-stage music into people's homes. Sidestep the pitfall of worship wars — fights over styles of music — by getting everyone involved in music. Once people start playing and singing music for themselves, you will be surprised how open they become. Shift your focus from the stadium —the Sunday service — to the farm team — homes and small-group settings. This means the quality of the music at the church service may suffer a bit at first, but soon you will reap all sorts of talented and willing players. Your job is not just to help the gifted get better but the ordinary get started.

If you are a pastor, you have a fundamental decision to make. Do you want your church service to be people's surrogate walk with God — the worship experience designed to carry them through the long drought of a whole week? Or do you want your worship service to be the culmination of all the individual, family, and small-group walks with God, and the culmination of the worshipping that has been going on all week in families, in cars, in small groups? If it is the latter, make it crystal clear to your staff and congregation that you are not as interested in what happens on Sunday morning as you are in what happens Monday through Saturday.

Start by finding out what is really going on in your church. How many of your people have personal devotions? How many have marriage devotions? How many have family devotions? (Visit www.WheresPhilip.com.) How many families sing during the week? How many play an instrument? What instruments? Do a survey and find out what you are up against.

Then create a strategy. Give everyone who has any music ability and leadership ability a copy of this book. Meet together and talk about what you are going to do. Make sure your strategy covers at least a year — this is not going to happen overnight. If you lack musical talent, start with a small strategy. If you have a lot of great players, come up with a bigger strategy. Give every family a copy of this book, and get people thinking about this language of praise. You will be surprised by what you can accomplish when you focus on something.

If you are a church planter, you have the advantage of starting fresh and not having to change years of habit. Emphasize the importance of music from day one. Get people memorizing a Song of the Month. Put the songs that you'll be singing for the next few weeks on a CD so the people can use and learn them at home. Use stickers or gift certificates as a reward for those who have practiced their instrument for three, six, or nine weeks straight, and recognize them in the service.

If you are a denominational executive, you are uniquely positioned to encourage the development of the inter-league play. Sponsor a song-writing contest. Give awards to churches with the highest percentage of their congregation involved in music. Sponsor "battle of the bands" events. Realize that the power of the denomination is its ability to honor and recognize growth in the desired direction.

It is time for you to decide what you are going to do about music in your life, in your family life, in the life of your church. It is time to make a plan and get started.

Review the chapters of the book that applied most to you and find ideas. Take a look at your life and see what people and resources can help you. Do this right away, before other distractions come along and you can't quite remember where you put this book. Then get started — play ball!

For information on music seminars or consultations for your church or denomination, contact selzinga@bibleleague.org.

THE FINAL WORD

This book was not written just to get you excited about music and the possibilities of music in your life and church. It was written to introduce you to a new paradigm, a new way of thinking about your relationship with God, your family and your mission in life.

This new way of thinking starts with the small before the big, gets you to see the church from the bottom up, not the top down, advocates using the average many before the talented few, believes in walking with God before talking about Him. This paradigm says, "Let's create playing fields where all people get a chance to play and develop at their own level." This paradigm asks, "Who knows what God has planned for you? Who knows what God can do through you?"

This book applies this way of thinking to music. If you want to see how this thinking plays out in other areas, check out the rest of this series:

The Secret to a Great Preaching Ministry
The Secret to a Great Discipleship Ministry
The Secret to a Great Evangelism Ministry
The Secret to a Great Leadership Ministry

ORDERING INFORMATION

The ideas in this book are meant to be shared with other people. Accordingly, we've made this book as inexpensive as possible so that you can afford to buy one for everyone in your band, choir, youth group, extended family, or church. You may purchase this book in lots of 10 for $2.99 apiece. Individual copies are only $3.99.

To order, call the Bible League at 1-800-871-5445, or visit us at http://www.wheresphilip.com/music.